Set Apart. Sold Out. Unashamed. I Don't Blend In—I Break Chains.

ENDORSEMENT

With bold faith, refreshing honesty, and a voice that rings true for her generation, Sarai Lokey invites readers into a deeper, unapologetic relationship with God. Holy Rebel is not just a devotional it's a rallying cry for teens who are ready to pray first, stand firm, and live fully for Christ. Sarai writes with both wisdom and wit, offering powerful truths in a way that's relatable, accessible, and rooted in Scripture. This is a book today's teens need and one they'll actually want to read.

—Amber O'Neal Johnston, author of Soul School and A Place to Belong

A DEVOTIONAL MANIFESTO FOR THE MISFITS, THE BOLD, AND THE UNASHAMED

HOLY REBEL

Set Apart. Sold Out. Unashamed.

I Don't Blend In- I Break Chains

Foreword by Amber O'Neal Johnston

"HOLY REBEL"

DEAR HOLY REBELS,

I'm Sarai. A fifteen-year-old girl who's seen many mountains, trials, and storms that would make some people shake in their boots, although it wasn't cold. A lot of rocks have been thrown at me, but they have all missed. One thing I have come to learn in my lifetime, which has been rather short, is that if anything, I would rather be judged by the world, because I don't want to be judged by God. God was there when I cried myself to sleep because I had pain in my hips. God was there when it felt like someone was pushing a dagger into my back, and when my bones felt as if they were trying to come out of my skin. God was there, the world wasn't, so the question became "Why should I, Children of God, give a care to what they think?" They can talk all day, but it won't erase the encounter I had with God during the hardest time of my life. You might be here because your mom made you pick up this book, maybe just because you received it as a gift or birthday present, perhaps the cover caught your eye, or just maybe you want to become closer to God. If you love God but aren't the shining beacon for Him in your friend group, community, household, wherever land you tread upon, but you want to be, this is the place for you. Now, I'm going to be straightforward and be scarily blunt with you. Being a Holy Rebel isn't easy. It's no kicks and giggles or strawberry smoothies while tanning on the beach. Becoming a new person and leaving some old ways behind can be hard, but I pray, despite what you have to leave behind, you stay and become a Holy Rebel, because you will gain so much more. What the world calls important and full of value just wants to destroy you and your light. Hey, do what some peers tell you to do, or allow social media to rob your purpose and be consumed with it and everyone on it. Drop this book and walk away. Go to party, continue your ways, and not give a care to putting more into God. BUT don't let people be the reason you don't pursue God, because he pursued you so much that He made sure your eyes landed on this book. Perhaps this book got your curiosity going when you saw the title, or maybe someone saw this and thought it would be good for you. Jesus pursued you and put you into the world for such a time as this. He makes no mistakes. Jesus created you in His image, intentionally decided when you would be born, what eras you would live in, and carefully thought through the even tiniest details, because He made you for it. And if you're here because you chose to be, a 'well done' at the heavenly gates is in store for you. There aren't many like us who choose to be here.

A lot of people don't understand and still can't comprehend why I'm all about Him. Well, if you don't know, now you know, this book is kind of a diary. So, guys, my secrets are out. Through this book, you will also learn why I am a Holy Rebel– the ins, outs, turns, all of it. I challenge you to read a chapter a day for the next ten days. I promise you will grow in God, gather some weapons for war, transform yourself into this person you only imagined you could be in some other universe, and step out, in full confidence, into the world differently, knowing you're on a mission, a God-given mission, by the end of this journey. You will be a whole new person! I'm not exaggerating. Most importantly, you will become the DREAM person in God you want to be. You will BECOME *that* Holy Rebel.

Our motto?

Set Apart. Sold Out. Unashamed. I Don't Blend In—I Break Chains.

P.S Just a quick warning, and don't say I didn't warn you– once you begin, the devil will be coming after you ten times as hard as he was before. He doesn't want you to discover the person who's been shut up in the closet. He prefers for you to be a suitcase shut up in the attic. He doesn't want you to read this book because he knows you are going to be an ASTEROID for the Kingdom when you're done. Once you know who you are and what power you carry, when you walk, speak, and enter a room, things are different and a glow and presence like no other can change any aura in the room. It's lifechanging, and you begin to hold a different standard for yourself because you know who you are and whose you are. Don't let NOTHING stop you. I can practically see the smirk on your face as the scoff comes out of your mouth. We'll see how you're doing come day three. Until then, stay strong and remember who your real enemy is. For the evils of this world aren't a problem, for it's Satan, who comes to steal, kill, and destroy. But remember, every time we take a step, we are walking on top of hell. It's not impossible to win. It's just impossible if you don't have a mustard seed of faith. Let's see if you make it through this book in the next ten days in one piece. Remember, we serve a God who can put all the broken pieces back together again. And we also serve a God who will use anything or anyone if He only has their 'yes'.

Through ten spiritually rich, truth-filled chapters, you'll explore what it means to stand strong in your identity as a Child of God while the world pulls you in every direction.

TABLE OF CONTENTS

PRAYER FIRST

I know that when you read the title of this chapter, you might have scoffed, thinking or even saying aloud, "Well, obviously." But the real question here isn't *what* to say when we pray, at least not the first question. If we're being honest, the first question is, "Do we really always pray *first*?"

Do we pray over our food?

Do we pray over our day?

Do we pray for our friends, upcoming tests, grandparents, the homeless, doctors– you name it?

Do we pray when trials and problems arise?

Yeah, I know it might seem like I'm taking it a little too far. But am I?

God cares about the small things we think about and the really big thoughts we spend hours pondering in our minds as well. We have an extraordinary gift: we can speak to God. But sometimes, we take it for granted.

I don't know about you, but I used to always go to my trusted friends and parents first. Or at least, there was a season when I would. If I'm being honest, there were many seasons when I went to people first, and not to God.

But over time, as seasons changed and the wind blew, I realized they weren't the answers to my problems. They couldn't even give me A-plus advice. I was turning to people who, like me, were human— created, limited, and in need of grace—instead of looking to God, the only One who's perfect, all-knowing, and able to sustain me. I was going to people when I should have been going to God. Don't get me wrong—talking through your problems with your parents isn't a bad thing, nor is asking them, or even your friends, for advice. I highly encourage talking to your parents or another trusted adult, because they've lived more years than we teens have, which means they know more.

Our friends, on the other hand, are great people to talk to and gain insight from. But do they truly know best? They are—or are around—our age and are still living and learning, just like we are. So realistically, how much more do they know?

And when we put it all on a scale, whose opinion do we value most—our friends' or God's? (The crickets are practically screaming in our ears at this point.). The main message that I

want you to know when you put down this book after reading chapter one is, "Prayer should NEVER be your LAST resort, but your
FIRST,". We have access to the King of Kings, Lord of Lords, Knower of the Future, and Creator of each of our stories that we uniquely and intentionally designed by the Designer. So I ask you, why don't we pray and seek Him first? He knows everything in divine detail. God created each of our stories before the beginning of time, and He made no mistake when He gave you such a trial at thirteen years old, a burden at fifteen years old, or an obstacle at seventeen years old. God was and is intentional with every move and decision He makes. He's a Master Chess Player who never makes a wrong move or decision He makes. So why not? Ask yourself, why not? Why *not* ask the Knower of All through a special communication system, uniquely crafted for us, something we all know, but rarely go to first, something called *prayer*. As normal as we make it sound, it's sacred, and as Holy Rebels for the Kingdom, we must know the power it holds. We must treat it and talk about it as such.

COULD IT BE OUR HABITS HOLDING US BACK?

Have you ever thought about that? Habits are the things we do out of routine. Have you gotten so used to going to friends or family for help that it's become a habit, while God has been pushed to the backseat... maybe even the trunk?

Maybe, over these next ten days, we need to break some cycles. Habits are things we do regularly. And after a while, habits transition into cycles, because they are patterns we repeat over a certain period. Is prayer something you turn to only as a last resort? Without even realizing it, when we push prayer to the back, we lessen its worth, importance, and value.

Do you truly know the power of prayer—and how much it can change things? For a long time, I didn't. I just prayed as it was one of the common things Christians do. I didn't make it personal until I was eleven years old. But once I discovered its power and began using it as my first response instead of my last, the mountains didn't seem so big. The lightning wasn't as scary. The thunder wasn't as loud.

Going to Jesus first and following His path can save us from heartache, pain, and anxiety. Let's make Him our first resort, not our last.

There's a woman named Hannah in the Bible who longed deeply for a child. **In 1 Samuel 1,** we read how she went to the temple and began to bawl her eyes out. She poured out her heart—her deepest wishes and desires—to God, pleading for a child. **Verse**

11 (NIV) says, *"And she made a vow, saying, 'LORD Almighty, if you will only look on your servant's misery and remember me, and not forget your servant but give her a son, then I will give him to the LORD for all the days of his life, and no razor will ever be used on his head."*

The text didn't need to plainly tell us whether Hannah had faith or if she was a lukewarm believer who only ran to God in times of need. Her words spoke volumes. She called herself "your servant," showing she was a willing vessel for God's Kingdom.

Hannah was a **Holy Rebel**—bold in faith, devoted in spirit, and surrendered in heart. She told God that if He gave her a son, she would raise him for His Kingdom and His work. And she did exactly that.

Side note to all the ladies out there: Hannah raised a Kingdom man. So, if you're still searching—and maybe even losing hope—wondering if any men are still being raised like that... just know there are some. Maybe. (Lol.)

Let's observe this story from the perspective of someone else who played a key role—Eli, the priest. He was simply doing his daily duties in the temple when Hannah arrived, probably with red, puffy eyes and blurry vision from crying so much.

It wasn't unusual for people to come in and pray, but Hannah did one thing that made Eli think she was out of her mind. To us, that one thing might not stand out—at least not at first.

Verses 12 and 13 (NIV) tell us: *"As she kept on praying to the LORD, Eli observed her mouth. Hannah was praying in her heart, and her lips were moving, but her voice was not heard. Eli thought she was drunk."*

UNUSUAL PRAYER AND A MISUNDERSTOOD HEART

These days, when people come to church to worship and pray, their actions aren't usually the center of attention. But back in biblical times, praying "in your head" was so uncommon that it could be seen as strange, or even a sign of drunkenness.

Eli, the priest, may have looked at Hannah with confusion or even disgust. Perhaps, with a firm tone, he said something like, "You're too drunk. Leave at once."

Hannah probably jumped in shock, embarrassed, drenched in tears, and stunned by the accusation. After all, she was pouring out her soul before God. She quickly explained her sorrow and the true nature of her silent prayer to the priest.

I like to think that, upon hearing her words, Eli's attitude shifted. As a man, but also as a servant of God, he may have softened. I can picture him responding with faith and compassion, giving her a firm nod and saying something along the lines of, *"God will provide."* Then, he sent her on her way, assuring her that God had heard her prayer and that her request would be fulfilled.

Long story short, Hannah had a son and named him Samuel. Unlike Abraham's wife, Sarai—and I'm not trying to be messy here, just stating facts—Hannah didn't ask her husband to sleep with a servant so she could finally have a child. She didn't take matters into her own hands. Instead, she took the matter to Jesus—the One who could do something about it.

She didn't go to her husband. She didn't run to a friend. She went to **God**, the Source and the Provider. Think about it: with all the problems we've faced, the burdens we've carried, the things we've needed, or those moments when we just needed someone to talk to... **have we gone to God first?** The first step in being a **Holy Rebel** is talking to God about everything—**first**.

You can't truly love or be obsessed with someone without knowing them deeply. If you want to take your relationship with God to the *Rebel* level, it starts with faith, trust, and prayer. That means telling Him everything **before** your best friend hears it. Before you text your cousin. Before you hit up the group chat.

Why call someone else when you could call the **Knower of All**? Sure, "Pookie" might speak back louder and be easier to see and hear. But that doesn't mean they have the best advice, or even know what you need. Jesus might be in Heaven, and His voice may be still and calm, but He knows **more** than your friends and parents ever will.

You can never go wrong with His guidance. Taking a moment or two to kneel at the feet of Jesus won't hurt anyone.

BUT HERE'S THE TRUTH:

How can you go right if you don't include Him?

Dear Jesus,

It's time for me to start coming to you when unexpected things come up in my life. You are the Knower of All, and I pray that You remind me, through trials and tribulations, to seek You and lay my requests at Your feet. You know what's best, and you want the best for me. My burdens and struggles are never a surprise to You, even though they often are to me. Holy Spirit, please remind me to run straight to my Father, to follow His voice, and to rely fully on His guidance.

I love You, and I pray this prayer in Your name.

Amen!

Being Bad for Christ,

Sarai

CHILD OF GOD

CONGRATULATIONS!

You made it through **Day One** and are now stepping into **Day Two** of becoming a better version of yourself. A *Holy Rebel* who will change every room you walk into!

You know, most people wouldn't even bother with a book like this. To be honest, I'm surprised you're still here. Some people would glance at the cover, *maybe* read the first page or two, then scoff and ask, "Who on earth would read something like this?"

Others—those who care too much about public opinion—are more invested in what their company, friends, or peers think. They're so afraid of being seen with a book like this, they walk right past it or toss it out. They worry about what others might think, say, or do, fueled by fear of criticism, judgment, or rejection.

But not you. I'm proud of you for choosing to be different, for wanting to grow closer to God. Being *set apart* isn't easy, but trust me—there's a greater reward for those who choose the narrow path.

No matter what people have said, or the thought-seeds the enemy has tried to plant in your mind, you're still here—growing stronger with every chapter. Now, I can't promise that you'll become a Holy Rebel—that's a decision only *you* can make. But what I *can* promise is this: I will give you the tools that can *transform* you into one. I know Jesus isn't trending—and He hasn't been for over two thousand years—but let me ask you this:

What's better? Being cool with people… or being in right standing with the Lord? You tell me. I'm not making that decision for you.

Matthew 7:13-14 (NIV) says: *"Enter through the narrow gate. For wide is the gate and broad is the road that leads to destruction, and many enter through it. But small is the gate and narrow the road that leads to life, and only a few find it."*

You've found the path this book is proof of that.

BUT HERE'S THE REAL QUESTION:

Are you going to walk it?

Yes, you're a Child of God **but do you know what that means?** I can only imagine the perplexed facial expression, the raised eyebrow, or maybe even the eye roll when you saw this chapter's title. Yes, I know I'm pointing out the obvious: you are, indeed, a Child of God.

But here's my question: how can you become a **Holy Rebel** if you don't know your value and importance? How can you truly love someone when you don't understand how deeply they love and care about you?

It's kind of like seeing a guy across the room and claiming, "I'm madly in love" or "I love him," but you barely know his name, favorite food, favorite show, or even what grade he's in.

(Sorry, am I being messy again? It's not intentional… but you get the point.)

Some people don't start holding their heads up until they *feel* worthy or good enough. But what if I told you the **King of Kings** looked at you and said, *"You are Mine"* and crowned you as His?

One of the foundational truths you must embrace before becoming a true Holy Rebel is knowing your **worth** and **significance** in the Kingdom. Because how can you call yourself His if you don't understand how special you are to Him?

Long ago, when the world was full of darkness, God thought about *you*. He imagined your eye color, your skin tone, your hair texture, and every detail of your physical features.

Psalm 139:14 (NIV) reminds us: ***"I praise you because I am fearfully and wonderfully made; your works are wonderful, I know that full well."***

The Bible also tells us that God created you in His image, meaning all of God's children look like Him, even if we have different skin tones or hair textures. You were created uniquely by your Father and are very special to Him. We are loved by God so much that, out of all of His creations, we are the only creation made in His image. That says a lot, doesn't it?

Luke 12:6-7 (NIV) says, *"Are not five sparrows sold for two pennies? Yet not one of them is forgotten by God. Indeed, the very hairs of your head are all numbered. Don't be afraid; you are worth more than many sparrows."*

He is so in love with you, He knows the exact number of hairs on your head. You are worth more than anything else to Him. So, no matter what the bullies tell you, or what social media deems worthy or important, the King of Kings the Man on the throne, the Creator, the Author, and the Finisher sees you as more valuable than anything else.

Screw the social media labels, for they are incomparable to the words and thoughts your Father has for you. Have you ever thought about how animals have been on Earth for centuries, and they all have a certain process and way of life? Cool, huh? The females do their thing and the males do theirs, but when it comes to humans—yeah, we have been reproducing the same way since the beginning of time but we all have different missions on this Earth. We all have a uniquely and specially designed purpose. You, Child of God, are now a part of His family, meaning He has something special for you to do before you leave this Earth. If no one has ever told you: **you are special**, and your worth is **unbreakable**. So special unlike the female giraffe who does the same thing as another female giraffe each woman of God has a special purpose, and each man of God has a special purpose.

You are so special that God gave you a way to talk to Him **prayer**. You are so special that God has provided you with a best friend, known as the **Holy Spirit**, to help you make the right decisions every day and to encourage you to do the right thing. He has provided you with **everything you need**, Child of God.

From now on, walk with your head held high. Don't cower at things that make your stomach churn, and don't let the devil's voice of negativity and discouragement take you off the path God has predestined for your life. The devil came to do three things: steal, kill, and destroy. He came to steal your hunger to know more about God, kill your faithfulness to God, and destroy your faith and every bit of you that wants to follow God's plan for your life. Don't let him.

It's an everyday fight against the devil and your faithfulness to God. **Ephesians 6:12 (NIV) says,** *"For our struggle is not against* *flesh and blood, but against the rulers, against the authorities, against the powers of this dark world and the spiritual forces of evil in the heavenly realms."*

One thing I have come to learn as a Christian is that the devil uses people to tear us down. The people who discourage you from reading your Bible, tease you for believing and loving God, and the ones who say all of those hurtful things that wear us down and cause us to rethink—are people who are being used as vessels for Satan's cruel plan.

Don't hate them or think badly of them. Pray for them, and then pray against their tactics and plans. Pray the six-word prayer—simple yet powerful: **"Lord, let Your will be done."**

We have no enemies on this earth. Our one and only enemy is Satan. We are **"not against flesh and blood"**, but against Satan and his cruelty. So, we have to wear the armor, Children of God.

You might be wondering—**armor?** Yeah, I know, it's pretty cool being a Child of God. We're kind of like superheroes. Plus, you didn't think you could go into battle with the evil one without armor, did you?

Ephesians 6:10-18 (NIV) says:

"Finally, be strong in the Lord and in His mighty power. Put on the full armor of God, so that you can take your stand against the devil's schemes". For our struggle is not against flesh and blood,

but against the rulers, against the authorities, against the powers of this dark world and the spiritual forces of evil in the heavenly realms. Therefore, put on the full armor of God, so that when the day of evil comes, you may be able to stand your ground, and after you have done everything, to stand. Stand firm then, with the belt of truth buckled around your waist, with the breastplate of righteousness in place, and with your feet fitted with the readiness that comes from the gospel of peace. In addition to all this, take up the shield of faith, with which you can extinguish all the flaming arrows of the evil one. Take the helmet of salvation and the sword of the Spirit, which is the word of God. And pray in the Spirit on all occasions with all kinds of prayers and requests. With this in mind, be alert and always keep on praying for all the Lord's people."

STANDING YOUR GROUND IN SPIRITUAL WARFARE

Standing your ground in spiritual warfare requires a few things:

1. **The Belt of Truth**

This is your weapon in war. Always speak the truth and encourage the truth, no matter what. No white lies allowed around here.

2. **The Breastplate of Righteousness**

No matter how hard it gets, do the right thing—even when faced with temptation. How? Pray and ask the Lord for help. Ask the

Holy Spirit to help you turn away from sin and show you another way out, because the Lord always provides a way.

3. **The Shoes of Peace**

Slide into your shoes and let no one and nothing take away the peace the Lord has given you—the peace that passes all understanding.

4. **The Shield of Faith**

Use your shield to protect yourself from all the claims that God isn't real, and from all the lies and tricks of the enemy that try to discourage and break your faith.

5. **The Helmet of Salvation**

Remember who saved you and made you clean, pure as a white sheep.

6. **The Sword of the Spirit**

The sword—your sword—is the Word of God. Your most powerful weapon in warfare is your Bible and the knowledge it contains. These verses also encourage you to pray regardless of the circumstances. The size of the request doesn't matter—what matters is your faith. Above all else, pray and look out for your brothers and sisters in Christ, also known as the Lord's people

When people ask, "Who are you?", we typically answer with our first name. I feel as if we, as people, believe that our name only has value or meaning because of how many awards or good deeds are tied to it. But I want you to know: answering with "A Child of

God" is MORE than enough. Your family doesn't have to be rich for you to be enough.

You don't have to wear fashionable clothing to be enough.

You don't have to speak three different languages to be enough.

Nor do you have to be the smartest kid in school to be enough. You are ENOUGH because God chose to die for your sins and call you His, **despite** what you have done and what you will do. You are **more than enough** because He has deemed you worthy, regardless of your sins and filth.

"Child of God" is not only a fact—it's a **fashion statement** and a **truth** that will never go unnoticed. You might catch someone off guard by answering, "A Child of God," because you're saying who you are and what you are. But what you're also implying—without saying—is that you know your value, your worth, and your importance, and you will allow **no one** or **nothing** to tear you down. Children of God, if you keep waiting for this world to accept you, you will be waiting your whole life, unhappy and full of everything *but* peace and joy.

YOU have to decide if being a **Child of God** is more than enough for you.

And if it is (which I hope it is), you are going to be **different**, **set apart**, and **chosen** for a special mission in His Kingdom.

Are you ready to walk into the Child of God you truly are?

If you are, then you can't tolerate certain things anymore. Do you have that one friend who likes cats and not dogs, so you typically don't bring dogs around them?

It's time for you, Children of God, to start **holding up a standard**. If you are a Child of God, you won't tolerate people saying false things about your God. You will **stand up for the Kingdom** with your weapon—**a.k.a. the Bible**.

If you are a Child of God, you won't play unholy music.

When people look at you, they will define you by what you **listen to**, **do**, and **say**. Never give anyone a chance to call you anything other than a **"Child of God."** People will use anything they can against you. **Don't** give them that opportunity—much less the satisfaction.

But remember—**don't be hard on yourself.**

You're still growing, just like me.

Dear Jesus,

Thank you for making me in Your image. Thank you for loving me and caring for me, despite the wrongdoings I have done. Please help me to remember my value, my worth, and my importance in a world full of darkness. I love You, and I am not afraid to be a Child of God. I know who I am, and in You, I am worthy, valued, and—most importantly—a Child of God. Please help me create a standard that you are happy with.

I love You, and I pray this prayer in Your name.
AMEN!

Being Bad for Christ,

Sarai

CHAPTER 3

THINKING LIKE A HOLY REBEL

People laugh at me all the time for only listening to Christian music. I get questioned, teased, and occasionally even a raised eyebrow with a "you-got-to-be-kidding" look. That's my personal favorite.

Some people don't believe me when I say music can be **detrimental** or **fundamental** to you. The music genre you choose to listen to is a choice you make every time you open your music app—and life is full of choices.

In one of my favorite movies, *Discarded Things*—which showcases two of my favorite actors of all time, Karen Abercrombie and Cameron Arnett—there's a scene that deeply spoke to me. It was a scene discussing what good music is, how music makes us feel, and what it does for us.

Another one of my favorite actors—yes, I got blessed to see three of my favorites all in one Christian film—Jemarcus Kilgore, who played Jalen, said an unforgettable line: *"We can listen to it when we want to, turn it off when we don't want to hear it anymore. We can either get something from it or get nothing at all; it just is. It lets us choose how we want to respond without telling us how we should."*

This line is very deep—and quite true. But one thing I want all of us to notice is that yes, music can speak to us or say nothing, but the devil will plant seeds for nothing to become something. Nothing can ever be "just is" with the devil sneaking around. Let that sit for a moment, reread it once or twice if need be. This line is very deep—and quite true. But one thing I want all of us to notice is that yes, music can speak to us or say nothing, but the devil will plant seeds for nothing to become something. Nothing can never be "just is" with the devil sneaking around.

Sure, music allows us to respond in any way, but the devil will create destructive thoughts, actions, or words based on how we feel or think about a thing. So yes, music **can** be detrimental if we are not mindful of what we are allowing our ears to hear.

Music of the world or music of the Kingdom— It's a choice that has to be made. The music you listen to can defeat the entire purpose you have in God's Kingdom. I'm not exaggerating—I'm keeping it honest. And the sinful tree in us humans can't handle that.

You might be called to lead people in your community or club to Christ. But how can you, when the lyrics start pulling your heart away from His plan for your life?

I promise you—if you just take the time to decipher a song or two of worldly music, you will find some hidden meanings you didn't even know were there! Worldly music is sneaky—like the devil—and we have to be on guard.

We have hidden prowlers all around us—such as spirits and demons, but that's a conversation for another day. Point is, Children of God, we must be very mindful, very aware, very demu-

Lemme stop—my bad. I'm a social media influencer. I can't help myself! But I think you get the point.

We have to be on alert with the type of music we digest and be mindful of our thoughts.

Before we go there, you know how when you eat too much junk food, your stomach starts to churn? It's the same way with our thoughts. When we start thinking about certain things, it can begin to twist or change our mindset.

Our thoughts are the **car door**, and our actions are the **gas pedal** that moves the vehicle, creating momentum. We may think that thinking about impure or bad things is fine. "They're just thoughts, right?"

Sure, they are—but those thoughts can end you up in places you didn't expect or didn't want to be in, because **thoughts are the first step to ACTION**.

Impure or misguided actions can lead us away from God's plan for our lives, and distance us from the Holy Spirit we long to have dwelling within us. We can be oblivious and ignorant and believe thoughts are just thoughts… Or we can change our mindset and clear our thoughts for the better. **Which route are you headed on?** You can only pick one, and I assure you: **God's way is MUCH better**. It's worth it—but I'll admit, it's hard. **But if I can do it, you can too.** It's the constant spiritual battle I spoke about earlier—between choosing the ways of Jesus and the path of Satan. So, what should we think about?

Paul tells us in Philippians 4:8 (NIV), *"Finally, brothers and sisters, whatever is true, whatever is noble, whatever is right, whatever is pure, whatever is lovely, whatever is admirable-if—if anything is excellent or praiseworthy—think about such things."*

The Bible tells us to think about true things—God's Word, for example. Every single verse in the Bible is true. God's Word is living and never dormant, even when the world shifts into a new era every few years.

We are also told to think about what is noble. After doing some research, I found that the origin of the word *noble* is the Latin word **gnobilis**, meaning *high-born*. Jesus Christ is on high. He is King, so we should focus on high-level things, not low-level thoughts.

Everything that is holy and acceptable in God's sight should be what we think about. Not the wrong things. We can fantasize, but it becomes a whole different story when we feel compelled to act on those fantasies. The first step to stopping those actions? **Shift your thinking.** You probably thought I was going to tell you to just stop thinking. But can we do that? Can we stop thinking? Uhm—I don't think so, no matter how hard we try. If anything, the thoughts get *louder* and more consistent.

God led me to ask a group of teens, may I interview them for Holy Rebel. He wanted me to get a variety of opinions, thoughts, and wisdom directly from His children. A group of bold teens who are Holy Rebels in their everyday lives, for God's army agreed to be willing vessels for my book's interview. We go on Zoom, and I asked them once we were all settled, "What do you do when you begin to have impure thoughts?". This was the first question of the interview. I saw a mixture of thinking faces, nervous faces, but I knew this was the beginning of something great. God told me lifechanging truths and words would be spoken on the call, and I believed it with all my heart. Ana, a fifteen-year-old from Virginia, answered within a few seconds, saying, "I've said this to Sarai many times: When you want to prove a point, prove it with a Bible verse, because no one can argue with that.". Ana's technique of rebuking the devil began with Bible verses and ended with them, because she believed, just like I do, that there is power in the Word of God and speaking it scares demons. Did you know that? Did you know your knowledge of the Word combined with your tongue can scare demons? Yeah, I know, we got some rebellious power lying on our tongues. Ana also believed that when we begin to have impure thoughts, we should speak to God. "Pursue a relationship with God because when you're in right standing with Him, you can hear Him.". Speaking to God, living life with God, will keep us so in love with Him, like a trance, that impure thoughts will be harder for the devil to drop. Ana encouraged, "Examine your life. If you open a door, you're opening it--not God". And that's facts Ivey, a fourteenyear-old girl from London, spoke up, adding, "Shift your attention to something positive and pray. 2 Timothy 2:22, "Flee the evil desires of youth and pursue righteousness, faith, love and peace, along with those who call on the Lord out of a pure heart.""

Ivey literally dropped a Holy Ghost bomb. I felt chill bumps all up my arms. When the creepy impure crawlers crawl into your mind and lay traps of lust, envy, we must flee from those thoughts. We must begin to pray, thinking about positive things.

Philippians 4:8 (NIV) says, "Finally, brothers and sisters, whatever is true, whatever is noble, whatever is right, whatever is pure, whatever is lovely, whatever is admirable—if anything is excellent or praiseworthy—think about such things.". We must rebuke those thoughts. Simply proclaiming the powerful name of "Jesus" can change things. Saying, "I rebuke you devil in the name of Jesus," will scare demons so much they'll go crying back to their mommas. Maisy, a sixteen-year-old girl from Georgia, said, "When I begin to have impure thoughts, I read my bible and study the word. I pray for the thoughts to go away and be replaced by thoughts that are honorable, true, and pure," I then moved on to ask, "What are you're five top Christian songs?". I personally believe music is a good distraction- depending on what type you listen to. Maisy said, "Gratitude by Brandon Lake, So Will I by Hillsong, and Graves into Gardens by Elevation Worship,". I can assure you all those songs will make you get up and praise until you pass out lol! Colin, a fourteen-year-old boy from Georgia, also added, "My favorite is Walk by Lecrae and Hulvey. I just love it. Music is just part of me at this point, especially Christian music. My entire family loves it, and a lot of my relatives play music." It's worth pointing out how much the people around us shape who we become. The things your loved ones and close friends do, say, and listen to—they start to rub off on you, whether you realize it or not. That's why it's so important to be mindful of who you keep in your circle. Holladay, a fifteen-year-old girl from Georgia, thoughtfully said, "I love Amen by Forrest Frank. I love what it talks about,". I obviously agreed (big

Forrest Frank fan—which is like the understatement of the century).

Sarai, a fourteen-year-old girl from Georgia, added, “I love “Amen” by Forrest Frank. I love what it talks about,”. I obviously agreed. Ana then added, “It’s Okay It’s Alright by Jimmy Cheo is good to!” As we’ve already discussed, listening to the right type of music can be fundamental or detrimental to your faith. When I was a lukewarm Christian, I loved Sorry Not Sorry by Demi Lovato, but as I got closer to God, I realized the lyrics weren’t so healthy and it actually went against things God’s Word said. I then asked, “Why do you like listening to music? What does it mean to you?”

Maisy said, “I always grew up in a very music-filled household because growing up, my mom always played on the worship team. My whole family is very musically talented and in my childhood church my mom played piano, and my dad played drums, and we always have these little 27 worship sections as a family in our piano room, and I sing, my dad plays drums, and my mom plays piano, so music has always meant a lot to me and my family.” Maisy’s response reminded me of home. I immediately felt so warm and happy on the inside. I was smiling as memories of me and my family laughing and goofing off flashed throughout my mind. This warmed my heart so much to know that families today still cherish and enjoy one another’s company. Family is important, and at the end of the day, they will show up when friends won't. Period.

Ana spoke up, saying, "Music is Biblical--worship music doesn't have to be hymnals". Ivey joined in, saying a valid and true statement, "Music curates a sense of community. It carries hope and it's not just you- it creates a community with people who like similar genres if not the same.

Beautifully said, and I couldn't have done it better. This was a beautiful addition to the chapter, and I really appreciate these Holy Rebels of God for keeping it biblical, relatable, and personal. Reread this section if you need to. Pray over it and add some of these amazing tools to your kit- you'll never know when you'll need them most. The following songs are great ones to add to your Holy playlist as well! Oceans (Where Feet May Fail) by Hillsong UNITED, Jireh by Elevation Worship & Maverick City Music, Goodness of God by Bethel Music, You Say by Lauren Daigle, and Way Maker by Sinach / Leeland.

Dear Jesus,

Thank you for giving us the power to renew our minds through Your Word. Help us to focus on things that are true, noble, right, pure, lovely, admirable, excellent, and praiseworthy. When impure or negative thoughts enter our minds, remind us to turn to You first. Strengthen our spiritual discipline so that we may resist the devil and draw closer to You. Thank you for the gift of music, which brings healing and draws us into deeper worship. Let the words we hear, and sing glorify You and help transform our hearts. Teach us to walk in Your truth and give us the strength to stand firm in the daily battle against spiritual darkness. Let our thoughts align with Your will, and may Your peace guard our hearts and minds in Christ Jesus.

I love you and I pray this in Your name. ***AMEN!***

Being Bad for Christ,
Sarai

NEW CREATURE

Don't you love seeing a snake slither away in its fresh, new outfit after its seasonal shed? Ooohhh, how about our friendly eight-legged creature? Remember that one time when you found a spider in your bathroom that you never had the guts to kill, but surprisingly, eight months later, you found another spider—possibly the same one—only slightly larger, but in your basement? You probably didn't think "new creature" right away. The hair on your arms might've risen, and your heart rate might've quickened as you stood there, frozen in shock. Your eyes widened, and your mind raced miles per hour as you tried to think of a plan.

Okay, at this point, you might be preparing to close this book, thinking I've lost my mind, which I can assure you I haven't (but only crazy people say that, right?).

When we put our faith in Jesus Christ, we don't literally shed our skin or physically grow. Instead, we're transformed in a spiritual sense, becoming new creatures. But if you don't know—now you know—most people stop there. Where is "there," exactly? Well, you know... most people put their faith in Jesus, become a Christian, possibly pick up the habit of attending church, prayer, reading their Bible—you know, the usual stuff.

But why just stop there?

I mean, God's Son, Jesus—literally the Prince of Peace and everything our hearts could ever want—came down and died to set us free, so that one day we can live in Heaven with the Father. By just doing the bare minimum, it's like taking that birthday present we wanted and maybe using it once or twice before it gets thrown in the closet or pushed under the bed.

Tell me why we aren't using the fullness of our gift? Because we are **a new creature**, a new person in Christ Jesus, we have the brightest and purest **light living and breathing inside of us**.

So, I don't know about you, but I want to use my gift to the **fullest extent**. I want to spend my life creating more disciples on Earth. I want to fish for men, not for fish. I want to do **eternal work that will last**, not things that will just pass away one day.

When we believe in Jesus, we have plants (commonly known as the Fruits of the Spirit) embedded inside of us: peace, love, joy, forgiveness—everything Jesus knew we would need and more.

So, why just use joy when you could access peace too?

As a **Holy Rebel**, you will sometimes be overcome with the feeling that you have so much on your plate that it makes you want to cry. Because, if we're being honest, the more we live for Jesus, the bigger our love for Him gets—and the more anxious we become, because we don't want to let Jesus down.

But the thing is, Children of God—something I've come to learn as all my hobbies (besides Beta Club) are centered on growing the Kingdom of God—is that as much as God wants me to dive into my purpose and calling, He never wants me to drown in a pool full of anxiety, anxiousness, and depression.

He doesn't want me to be arrested by these evil fruits. And he doesn't want you to be arrested either. So today, Day 4, is the day I declare in Jesus' name that you walk out of your prison cell. When I was interviewing the chosen individuals for Holy Rebel, I asked them, "How you keep your peace when you have a lot on your plate? Ivey, a fourteen-year-old Holy Rebel from London, reflected for a moment before saying, "Regularly reading and reflecting on the Bible verses that speak of peace. Matthew 11:28-30 (RSV), "Come to me, all you who are weary and burdened, and I will give you rest. Take my yoke upon you and learn from me, for I am gentle and humble in heart, and you will find rest for your souls. For my yoke is easy and my burden is light." It reminds me of the peace, comfort, and reassurance God provides when I need it,". Ivey's picking of that verse left me in awe as it reminded me that Jesus is a resting place for all who love Him. He doesn't just care about us when we are trending, He cares for when we are tired and stuck too. He cares when we are on fire for Him and even when we have lost our way. Holladay, a fifteen-year-old girl from Georgia, shared something practical—words of wisdom for our Holy Rebel toolbelt. "I like to write or pray when I'm not home and don't have my Bible with me.". I want you to know Holy Rebel, praying or reading your Bible isn't more important than the other- they are all equal and they both carry the same living power.

Maisy said, voice full of honesty, "I keep my peace by just praying whenever I feel worried and talking to my mom. She gives really good advice, and she knows how to help me when I'm stressed,". As much as we like to keep our parents "out of our business", they have a lot of knowledge and wisdom, and I truly believe, like Maisy, it's good and healthy to keep them involved—if not safe.
Ana, the last to answer, said something that knocked the wind out of me.
"Isaiah 26:3 (NIV) says, "You will keep in perfect peace those whose minds are steadfast, because they trust in you." Whenever I get busy, I have to remember I'm under grace, not law. It's better for me to put something off than lose my peace" WHAT A WORD. Holy Rebel, let me make this very clear to you, choosing

to walk the pace of peace is better for you spiritually, physically, mentally, and emotionally than running yourself into the ground. No one is more important than YOU. You can't help others if you don't help YOURSELF. You can't show up with your best if you don't take care of yourself first. Period. Your to-do list isn't worth losing your mind. Was that clear enough? Yes, I know, I'm not funny lol.

Ana then went on to say, "Hey, maybe I have five things to do today, if I can only do three and I keep my peace, that is far more valuable than those tasks getting done,".

PREACH PASTOR PREACH. Guys, listen, if you run yourself into the ground, God will grab you, sit you down, and literally make you do nothing. He will stop everything. If you want to be used by God, you have to know when to work and when to chill. That's not something that has always been easy for me as a rebellious Holy Rebel, but I had to learn quickly. Ana then began to share a personal story. In 2021, she had a death scare occur within her family when her mom's lung capacity had dropped to thirty percent. Her mom had recently gotten COVID-19, but at the time, they did not know it. The doctors weren't sure how she was still alive, and they sent her home with an oxygen tank. Her mother heard the voice of God tell her to turn it off, and years later, she's alive and well today, being a Proverbs 31 momma to her beautiful family in Virginia. Ana expressed how her dad told her to pray when they were at the hospital, but she was so emotional she couldn't so she begin to speak in tongues and she trusted that God heard her, despite her plate being an emotional heavy wreck. After taking a moment to let all of these wonderful words of wisdom and knowledge sit, I then asked my second question. "What does peace mean to you?". Ana spoke first as she felt a word enter her from the Holy Spirit. "Peace is a freedom from disturbance". Can I get an 'Amen'? As soon as she said this I thought of Forrest Frank's song "No Lounger Bound". Go give it a lesson after this chapter. Ana then went on to say, "When you're working under stress, your work isn't going to be as effective,". At this moment, I sat up, walked away from my computer. I needed a minute to let the Holy Spirit calm me. I had chill bumps as I shook my head muttering, "My God, my God,". And she's not wrong- when you're stressed, you aren't as careful and especially not at peace. But God wants us to have peace, He doesn't like it when we are stressed out. Maisy said, "To me peace means to give every thought that disrupts your peace to God and not worrying about things that you can't control. I believe it is our job as Christians to KEEP AND MAINTAIN the peace as best as we can which means staying out of drama, not being an instigator, not wearing revealing outfits that will cause unwanted attention to ourselves, not engaging in conversations we know will end badly etc.". All I got to say is facts. Half the stuff we get caught up in is because we opened the door to it. And it could've been shut if we asked God what to say and do, not just speak without Heavenly consent.

Dear Jesus,

Thank You for coming for me. Thank You for coming to save me when I didn't quite know yet that I needed saving. You're so loving and merciful that it's beyond comprehension why You suffered and gave Your all for people just like me.

I've decided today that You make living for You worth it in every aspect of my life. I pray that You breathe Your peace into me, touch me with Your love and healing, and ignite a fire in my bones for You.

I love You, and I pray this prayer in Your name.
AMEN!

Being Bad for Christ,
Sarai

I WANNA BE USED BY YOU

I always admired people who allowed the Lord to use their lives for His Kingdom. It's a somewhat lonely walk that often leaves you questioning your choices—trust me, I know. Not the questioning part—that's a rare one for me—but the lonely part. For many seasons, although I had friends, sometimes life was lonely, as no one I knew was doing the type of work I was doing. They didn't understand it, and sometimes they questioned it.

Thankfully, my faith was built on an unshakable rock—**Jesus**—so it didn't bother me. Not much, anyhow. Choosing God sets you apart, and it definitely doesn't get you into the "cool crowd." People leave when you choose Jesus. People talk. A lot of scary things happen, making you question if it's all worth it—that type of stuff. **You, Child of God, are here because you've decided it's all worth it.**

Let me tell you—**IT IS**. It's so worth it that God's *"Well done, my good and faithful servant"* at Heaven's gates is gonna bring some of us to tears. I can't wait to hear it! Actually… I can, because I'm still here—and you are too— which means one thing and one thing only: **He's not done with us. Not yet.**

So, some people think God is in control. I'm one of those people. Some people think God CONTROLS people. Uhm, no. He isn't some mastermind genius— Actually yes, He is. He created the whole universe in like six days. No one else has that on their résumé.

Anyway, the point is, **that you have to be a willing VESSEL for God to use**. He had a purpose in mind for you when He created you, but that doesn't mean you were automatically going to follow through with it.

The Bible tells us God gives us a choice: to serve Him or serve the world. We aren't forced to do anything. We just have to pick. But be advised: this isn't Reese's or Kisses. This is life or death.

John 15:19 (NIV) says, *"If you belonged to the world, it would love you as its own. As it is, you do not belong to the world, but I have chosen you out of the world. That is why the world hates you."* The Bible is still a living and active Word to this day, and it is telling us—we aren't owned by or a part of the world. That's why it is against us. We are of God's creation—His masterpiece—that He has chosen. The world hates us because they **HATE** Jesus. Guys, they hated Him first. Disliked Him so much they killed Him on the cross! So of course, the world is going to hate His children because we are of Him.

The Word says in Psalm 91:7 (NIV), *"A thousand may fall at your side, ten thousand at your right hand, but it will not come near you."*

If you choose God, fires and storms may rise around you—even within your household—but they will not consume you, for the Lord your God watches over you. This verse also tells us that people are going to hate us, mock us, 'disown' us, neglect us—who said we need them when we have a **King** on our behalf—and so much more! Let me tell you, they can come **this close**, but they **WON'T** be able to touch you! God has His angels underneath you, on top of you, and on each of your sides. Trust this information and stand on this information.

There's this story in the Bible that can be found in **John 8 (NIV).** Specifically, verses **5 through 8**. In the middle of teaching in the temple, the Jews and Pharisees brought a woman guilty of adultery to Jesus. **The verses tell us:** "In the Law Moses commanded us to stone such women. Now what do you say?"

They were using this question as a trap, in order to have a basis for accusing him. But Jesus bent down and started to write on the ground with his finger. When they kept on questioning him, he straightened up and said to them, "Let any one of you who is without sin be the first to throw a stone at her." Again, he stooped down and wrote on the ground."

Guys, when I tell you our Jesus was a "**He says, and no follow-up questions**" type of guy, that's what He was! Have you ever met someone who, whenever they say something, makes everyone quiet? No one even dares to speak? That's what Jesus did in that moment because **He's the man**.

But no, for real—above all else—what I want us to catch in this moment is this: (And disregard that she was caught in the act of something ungodly and immoral.) Take into consideration that **Jesus stood up for her**. These men were going to throw stones at her. **STONES**. Can you imagine a stone hitting your body? No—scratch that—**multiple stones**. When someone throws something intentionally, it can hurt ten times worse. Jesus said, *If you haven't sinned, be the first to stone her.*

I don't know about you, but I can imagine the smirks dropping from the scribes' and Pharisees' faces because they were also trying to trick Jesus. I can see their eyes being hit with recognition that they couldn't stone her. I told you that story because I want you to know: People will come **THIS** close, but they **can't touch you**, because **Jesus has His hand over you**. Our enemies—they are slick, and some are witty—but no one can outplay our **Master Chess Player**, our **Lord**, our **man, Jesus Christ**. I'm sure we all know the great **David and Goliath** story. David— the underdog, scrawny little kid. All he had were stones and a slingshot. At least, that's all the mere onlooker saw. They didn't see his secret weapon. Can't blame them—most don't.

They didn't see that he had the **King of Kings** on his side. Onlookers didn't see **Jesus**—well, at first, at least. Goliath, on the other hand—built like Dwayne Johnson, aka **The Rock**—was super tall. Probably had a nice chiseled jaw, and nice refined biceps... everyone probably felt overly confident that he could take down this little kid.

Well, what people seem to always forget—and it's about time we let the world know (agreed?)—is that when you put **God** into the equation, **ANY and EVERYTHING is POSSIBLE**. Let's just say, **they** (David and God) shut it down.

1 Samuel 17:45 (NIV) tells us before they had the victory: *"David said to the Philistine, 'You come against me with sword and spear and javelin, but I come against you in the name of the LORD Almighty, the God of the armies of Israel, whom you have defied.'"* I don't know about you, but after that, one thing became very clear to me:

The name of Jesus has more power than a spear or any other weapon combined.

I think it's safe to say we now understand, **Psalm 91:7 (NIV),** *"A thousand may fall at your side, ten thousand at your right hand, but it will not come near you."*—**truer than ever**. We know what it means on a deeper level now.

Now that we know God will protect us if we choose to be vessels, let's take a look at one person in particular whom God used **MIGHTILY** because she was a willing vessel—**Esther**.

Esther was a beautiful young girl who had a tragic past. Her parents died, and she moved in with her loving cousin, Mordecai. After a series of events that included a pampering process of a year, being taken into the king's presence, and more, she was crowned the Queen of Persia.

Now, Haman, one of the king's officials who was officially promoted to prime minister, had history. All the bad guys do, right? As Haman was approaching the gates, every royal servant bowed down to him—except for Mordecai, for he only bowed down to God. Haman became furious. He crafted a plan and manipulated and tricked the king into doing something unchangeable.

One day, Esther received an alarming message from her cousin Mordecai through one of her servants. *Esther 4:6–9 days*—and let me take a small moment to encourage you to pull out your own

Bible and read these living words,*"So Hathak went out to Mordecai in the open square of the city in front of the king's gate. Mordecai told him everything that had happened to him, including the exact amount of money Haman had promised to pay into the royal treasury for the destruction of the Jews. He also gave him a copy of the text of the edict for their annihilation, which had been published in Susa, to show to Esther and explain it to her, and he told him to instruct her to go into the king's presence to beg for mercy and plead with him for her people. Hathak went back and reported to Esther what Mordecai had said."*

Haman was angered so much by Mordecai's rebellion that he asked King Xerxes to make a decree and let it be known in all the land— the annihilation of the Jews. I don't know about you, but despite my feelings for one person, I wouldn't sentence them **and** their people to death! Like, you seriously have a heart of stone.
As soon as the people heard, Mordecai ran to the palace to make Esther aware. He begged her to go to the king and plead for their people's lives. I can't imagine Esther's face. I can't imagine her heart. I'm sure her breath stopped for a moment, and her face was stricken with sadness and grief. Her servant tells her heart-breaking, astonishing news. Her face probably grew pale, her mouth slightly ajar, shaking her head slowly. It probably seemed surreal.

As she thought about it more and more, a lightbulb flicked on in her head. She couldn't go to the king. It wasn't that she didn't want to, but if she went into the king's presence without being summoned, it could be "Three, two, one—off with her head!" Sorry, this isn't a time for jokes. Anyway, in order to see the king, you typically had to be summoned by him. If she went to see the king and he didn't raise his scepter in consent, she could be put to death. And not just that—but Esther had a secret Mordecai once urged her to keep: she was a Jew.

Yeah, trust me, this is a book I would read over and over again. It could be a bestseller.

Esther 4:12–14 says: *"When Esther's words were reported to Mordecai, he sent back this answer: 'Do not think that because you are in the king's house you alone of all the Jews will escape. For if you remain silent at this time, relief and deliverance for the Jews will arise from another place, but you and your father's family will perish. And who knows but that you have come to your royal position for such a time as this"?*

I can practically hear Mordecai's voice—full of seriousness, realness, realization, consideration—when he told the servant to tell Esther: *just because you are the queen doesn't mean you are exempt from this death sentence of a decree.*

What a blow, am I right? Real, but a blow. If you choose to *"remain silent"* during all of this havoc, our *"relief and deliverance"* will come from somewhere else—but you and your bloodline *"will perish."* I don't know what God's plans are, but what if the whole purpose of you being chosen by King Xerxes as the new queen—a royal position—was *"for such a time as this"?* It never fails to amaze me at the word choices Mordecai used. I would do almost anything to hear his tone of voice as he said that to the servant. They're not just thought-provoking words—they're emotionally impacting. Words you can't stop thinking about. Words you will feel all your days if you don't act.

After a few days of fasting—wait, no—I'm not telling what's next. Sorry! I'm sure you're feeling that same feeling you get when Mom calls you down for dinner or Dad asks you to do chores right when you get to the climax of a good story or show.

Nonetheless, we have to stop for a moment, sit, and ponder on this amazing thing called **fasting**. Before doing anything, Esther told Mordecai to tell the people: *fast with me for three days*. As they fasted, Esther prayed for a beautiful thing called **salvation**. I think this picture shows us how important it is to go to God when we are in the middle of a trial. It shows that going to God should always be our **first resort**, never our last. And yes, I'm going to keep pushing that truck till the end of our journey—just so you know.

After three days, Esther pulled herself together, got ready and fit like a true queen, and went to see the king. **Pure poise, elegance, and grace in every step.** I can't imagine the anxiety and worry that crept into her head. I'm sure butterflies filled her stomach and she had goosebumps on her arms.

Well, I think—and the Bible confirms it—that it's safe to say, Esther wasn't put to death. The king saw her and was pleased with her. I can't imagine the shaky breath that went out of her mouth when the king raised his scepter to her. I'm sure she then smiled the widest smile she had ever displayed.

After two dinners with the king and Haman, Esther told the king what was troubling her.

Long story short—Haman was hung on the same gallows he had created for Mordecai (the nerve, am I right?), and the Jews were safe and sound by God's hedge of protection. This is a **"But God"** story! Of course, if Esther hadn't done it, God would have used someone else. Unlike us, He puts His eggs in multiple baskets—but that's a story for another day. **What we need to see and remember here is:** that Esther consumed the problem at hand, digested it through three days of intentional prayer while fasting—instead of jumping at the first thing her mind said to do—and then went to see the king. She made herself a WILLING vessel.

Jesus will never force you to work or follow Him: A person who **wants** to be used by God has to fully surrender themselves.

Esther surrendered by going into a three-day fast to hear and talk with God through prayer.

Surrendering yourself fully to God is **not** a one-time thing—believe me. You have to **constantly** do it, because there is a **constant spiritual war** between the flesh and the spirit. Being a willing vessel is a **twenty-four-hour** commitment—you don't get the weekends off. God gives assignments, and there are deadlines. If Esther didn't do it, He would have found someone else—I can assure you of that. If you truly want to do this **Holy Rebel** thing, you have to **SURRENDER**. Hey, look at you! You made it halfway through this book, which means you're becoming the new you already. I'm sure you, your family, your friends—people who mean the world to you—can see the difference. **I'm proud of you**, but hey, it isn't over yet. **See you in the next half!**

Dear Jesus,

Thank You for this knowledgeable, thought-provoking chapter— even if Sarai took her sweet time with it. You know she's passionate! Please help me surrender myself to You every single day. I wanna be used by You, and in order for that to happen, I have to let go of me and fully embrace Your plan. Please help me become the child of God—**the HOLY REBEL**—who chooses to be used by You. I want to be a Holy Rebel who receives and completes his/her assignments.

I love You, and I pray this prayer in Your name.

AMEN!

Being Bad for Christ,

Sarai

WHEN EVERYTHING YOU DO IS ABOUT G-O-D

Have you ever met someone whom you truly believe has *"no life"*? Have you ever met a teen who spends all of their time, outside of school and family activities, doing things that benefit the Kingdom?

Really? Is that a *no*? Surprising.

Well, meet **Sarai Lokey**. A teenage girl who has a spiritually led blog, *Generation of Young Believers*; thriving social media pages where she produces Christian content of all kinds; she's a speaker, an actress for Christ, and—probably her favorite of all—speaking the Word and writing books.

She's a published author of *McVee and the Spirit* and now… at this point, you might've turned back to the front cover of this book thinking, *"Wait, isn't the author Sarai Lokey?"* Yeah, it's me, guys. Haha.

It's not that my parents forced me to do everything that's ministry— it's just that nothing else seemed to be ***my thing***. Nothing set a fire under my feet, nothing kept me up at night, nothing inspired me— except for writing books for the glory of God, speaking about my Father's goodness and bringing transformative and revelatory words to His people, acting to produce fruitful content for the Kingdom, and all the other stuff I do.

Am I saying that as a Holy Rebel, everything you do has to be about Christ? No, not at all. But because you are a Holy Rebel, you have the living Word of God inside you, and you can't allow all of your other passions and talents to **dormant** the Holy Spirit in you. What I *am* saying is: no matter what you do—play sports, be president of your Beta Club, mathematician queen, member of a Boy Scouts troop, Robotics Champion—**make sure you do everything for the glory of God**. God gave us our minds, gifts, and talents, so why not honor Him for what He gave us?

You know, if you read any of the acknowledgments in my books, you'll see me refer to the finished project as *"We did it!"* A lot of you may be confused by that, as the cover says it was written by one person: Sarai Lokey (me). Well, I couldn't have done it without God. He gave me the ideas, details, character names, plot twists— everything. Why take credit for something I didn't even come up with?

It's like offering a solution or baking cookies for someone, but the idea wasn't originally yours—you just took it from someone else. It's wrong when you think about it. So, it's never an *"I did it,"* it's always a *"We did it."*

Everything I do—besides Beta Club and piano—is centered on Christ. But even in those atmospheres, I still exhibit Christ in the way I talk, act, and handle situations. Everything I do is a **replication of Christ**, and I don't know about you, but *I wanna make my Daddy look good.*

And it starts with reflection, then cleaning out my heart, and then producing good fruit—**fruit my Father would want to eat**.

Today's chapter is short—not going to hit you guys with a doozy after yesterday, lol. I love you and am so proud! **Four more days to go, Holy Rebel**.

Before we go, I want to take a moment to remind you of our motto:

Rather be judged by the world than face judgment from God. Can I get an *AMEN*?

Being Bad for Christ,

Sarai

KNOWING YOUR WEAPON

AS HOLY REBELS, DO WE HAVE WEAPONS?

Uhm, yes! We have a weapon that has been around for **years** but is still **alive**, **active**, and just as **powerful**. Meet the **Bible**.

In Chapter 2, we discussed the **armor** we are supposed to wear as Holy Rebels, but today I want to touch on our **weapon**. How do we use our Bible? And why do we consider it a weapon?

When storms and trials arrive in our lives—such as getting bullied at school, dealing with a group of people in your club who don't like you, or treating that one girl in Girl Scouts with kindness even when she's blatantly rude—we need our weapon, **our Bible**, to help us get through it.

Our Bible is our **map to success**, our **guide** to ensure that—if we follow it—we don't go down the wrong path. Which, in other words, is the **Devil's path**.

I don't know about you, but I want to use my weapon to the **fullest extent**! We have the **Book of Life** at our disposal—so why not take it and use it until we can't use it anymore?

Which, if I'm being fully honest, it can **never** go out of use.

Hebrews 4:12 says,

"For the word of God is quick, powerful, and sharper than any twoedged sword, piercing even to the dividing asunder of soul and spirit, and of the joints and marrow, and is a discerner of the thoughts and intents of the heart."

I want to give you a list, and I want you to make a decision.

Reread what I just said: I want to give you a list—so I'm going to give you a list. And I want you to make a decision. I'm not going to force you to do anything—I literally won't. Like, what can I do? Jump through these pages like a Holy Ninja and grab your neck until you do it.

Nah—I'm not built like that. Plus, it's not possible. And even if I could, I wouldn't. I'm not.

Choosing Christ for yourself is a personal decision—one that I, your parents, or your friends can't make for you. I want to encourage you to take a look, pray over the list, and choose **one to three books of the Bible** to read. Not all at once, but rotate through them over the course of a month. The more you read, the more knowledge you'll gain. Like me, you'll find yourself in situations, and all of a sudden, you'll begin quoting Bible verses meant for **you**—verses for encouragement, anxiety, peace, and wisdom.

Once you pick your book or books, I want you to read only **five to eight verses a day**. Mark the top of the page in your notebook or journal like this:

Entry 1 - Date - Book - Chapter: Verses

I do this every day—sometimes two to three times if I have the time! I also watch sermons and follow Bible reading plans outside of these entries, so in total, I spend about an hour with God each day. But my entries? They're personal.

I **dare you** to try this for a month. Seek God and listen to His voice. Some days, He'll tell me to read three verses. On other days, ten. When I'm tired, He understands and might just tell me to pray and not do an entry. Be **attuned** to God.

God wants you.

The question is:

"Do you want Him"?

OLD TESTAMENT (39 BOOKS)

The Law (Pentateuch / Torah)

Genesis – Book of Beginnings: Creation, Fall, Flood, Patriarchs

Exodus – Book of Deliverance: Israel's escape from Egypt

Leviticus – Book of Holiness: Laws for worship and holy living

Numbers – Book of Wanderings: Israel's 40 years in the wilderness

Deuteronomy – Book of Remembrance: Moses' final sermons before entering the Promised Land

History (Israel's Story)

Joshua – Conquest of the Promised Land

Judges – Cycles of sin, oppression, and deliverance

Ruth – Book of Redemption: God's providence through loyalty and love

1 Samuel – Israel's first kings: Saul and David's beginnings

2 Samuel – David's reign as king

1 Kings – Solomon's reign and the kingdom's division

2 Kings – Decline and fall of Israel and Judah

1 Chronicles – David's reign with focus on temple worship

2 Chronicles – Focus on Judah's kings and temple history

Ezra – Return from exile and rebuilding the temple

Nehemiah – Rebuilding Jerusalem's walls

Esther – God's providential protection of His people

Wisdom & Poetry

Job – Book of Suffering and God's Sovereignty

Psalms – Book of Praise and Prayer

Proverbs – Book of Wisdom for Daily Living

Ecclesiastes – Book of Meaning: Life without God is meaningless

Song of Solomon – Book of Love: Marriage and intimate love as a picture of God's love

Major Prophets

Isaiah – Book of Salvation and Messianic Prophecy

Jeremiah – Book of Warnings and Judgment
Lamentations – Book of Grief over Jerusalem's Fall

Ezekiel – Book of Restoration and God's Glory

Daniel – Book of Faithfulness and End-Time Visions

Minor Prophets (Shorter Prophetic Books)

Hosea – God's Love for Unfaithful People

Joel – The Day of the Lord and Repentance

Amos – Justice for the Oppressed

Obadiah – Judgment on Edom

Jonah – Mercy for the Repentant (Even Enemies)

Micah – Judgment and Hope for Israel

Nahum – God's Judgment on Nineveh

Habakkuk – Wrestling with God's Justice
Zephaniah – Day of the Lord and Restoration

Haggai – Rebuilding the Temple

Zechariah – Encouragement and Future Glory

Malachi – Final Call to Return to God

📖 NEW TESTAMENT (27 BOOKS)

Gospels (Life of Jesus)

Matthew – Jesus as the Jewish Messiah

Mark – Jesus as the Suffering Servant

Luke – Jesus as the Perfect Savior (Historical and detailed)

John – Jesus as the Son of God (Emphasis on belief)

History

Acts – Birth and Growth of the Early Church

Paul's Letters (to Churches and Individuals)

Romans – Salvation by Faith

1 Corinthians – Addressing Church Issues

2 Corinthians – Defense of Paul's Ministry

Galatians – Freedom in Christ

Ephesians – Unity in the Body of Christ

Philippians – Joy in All Circumstances

Colossians – Supremacy of Christ

1 Thessalonians – Hope and Christ's Return

2 Thessalonians – Clarifying the End Times

1 Timothy – Instructions for Church Leaders

2 Timothy – Paul's Final Words of Faith

Titus – Sound Doctrine and Good Works

Philemon – Forgiveness and Reconciliation

General Letters

Hebrews – Jesus as the Fulfillment of the Old Covenant

James – Faith That Works

1 Peter – Hope Through Suffering

2 Peter – Warning Against False Teachers

1 John – Love and Assurance of Salvation

2 John – Truth and Love

3 John – Support for God's Workers

Jude – Contending for the Faith

Prophecy

Revelation – Final Victory of Christ and Eternal Hope

Holy Rebels don't fight with fists—they fight with faith. And our faith grows every time we open our Bible, the greatest weapon of all.

Dear Jesus,

Thank you for this day. Please set a fire in my stomach that urges me to know my weapon. Please bring to my remembrance Your Word—Your Truth—in the midst of the storms life brings. Although life is always lifin', I pray I remember my God is still God despite the storm I'm facing. The storm might look scary, because I can see it with my own two eyes, but I ask you, Holy Spirit, to help me remember who's on the throne and who's in control.

I love you and I pray this prayer in your name.
AMEN!

Being Bad for Christ,
Sarai

HOLY REBEL STRUGGLES

If I had to be honest, which I live by honesty, one of my personal Holy Rebel struggles is the rare little voice in the back of my head wondering why I'm not normal. Sometimes it's so hard to do what I do, especially when I discuss certain topics with peers, and they don't get it or can't offer advice. Many of my peers aren't on the same level with Christ as I am and that has been difficult, but you know what has helped? Finding a character in the Bible I can relate to and knowing my Father's proud of me and has a special plan just for me. I'm set apart and at the end of the day I wouldn't rather anything else. For if my Father's happy, I would rather be proudly on assignment than be understood by the world, who won't care for me after I'm dead. That's just the hard truth.

And, you know, it's not that I necessarily wanted to relate to someone—I wanted to be reminded (although I didn't realize it until after the revelation) that God wasn't through with me yet.

Even though I constantly reminded myself of that truth and rebuked the devil in Jesus' name, it didn't stop the demons from whispering lies.

I want to tell you guys about my first experience at a youth group where I truly felt the presence of God. I didn't expect much—just a few laughs with my good friends, a moment to worship and get lost in the Spirit, and maybe something in the message that resonated with me.

One thing I will say is this: when you reach a certain point in your relationship with Christ, it becomes harder to sit in a youth group service because the lessons no longer challenge you. I've been in that season for a few years, and it's been tough. I withdrew. I started sitting in the sanctuary instead—where my fire grew, my spirit was awakened, and my relationship with God was challenged.

But despite that change, I still missed being part of a youth group. My friends had been begging me for nearly a year to attend their youth group on a Sunday night. We live an hour and fifteen minutes apart, so it was always difficult. But one Sunday, we finally made the drive.

I stepped out of the car and ran to hug my friends. I wore a pleasant smile, but my spirit wasn't expecting a night full of surprises—much less tears and a revelation.

I met my friends' youth leader, Gabby, and the youth pastor, Pastor Geanna. They were genuinely kind. Gabby was stunning and so sweet in the Spirit. Pastor Geanna was down to earth and very energetic.

After a game of football, everyone was called inside for worship and the message.

For the first time at a youth group, during worship, I encountered the Holy Spirit in a way I had never experienced before. It was heavy—as if He wasn't just in me, but in the air all around me. I remember halfway through one song, I fell to my knees and lifted my hands. Everyone was around me—I was closest to the stage—but I was lost in a trance. It was just me and the Holy Spirit. Halfway through, my back started hurting. And that's when I knew: this place, these people—they knew God and loved Him deeply.

Why is this significant?

I was diagnosed with scoliosis at age twelve. Every time I worshiped in the sanctuary, my back and hips would begin to ache with excruciating pain—to the point where I had to leave the room and cry. After a few moments, the pain would pass.

So yes, I went back to my seat in the front row and sat down—but did I leave the room? Not in a million years.

Did I stop worshiping? Not in a million years.

I raised my hands. I kept crying. I continued to praise, despite my pain.

Most of the kids around me were also worshiping, and it looked so serene and intimate. I was already overwhelmed... and then came the message.

It was called **"Grad Szn."**

A lot of that message stuck with me, but one thing stood out loud and clear:

"The blessing follows endurance."

And if it takes everything in you to keep going—to keep enduring— do it.

Because **God doesn't break His promises**; He's just on a different timeline than we are.

During the entire message, I kept saying "Amen" aloud, lifting my hands to receive the Word, and clapping. I was that one kid in the front row "doing the most." But I wasn't just present—I was obsessed with the Spirit that evening. I leaned forward in my seat, trying to catch every single word.

I say all of this to remind you: **Holy Rebel struggles are real.**

But after years of waiting, God will answer a prayer.

That message Pastor Geanna preached was such confirmation for me. At the time, I had been querying literary agents for my Christian YA novels for months, hoping for an offer of representation. I've continued to keep my faith, writing, and praying.

I have **two completed manuscripts** on my desktop, and another one is almost finished. I don't know when God is going to answer my prayer and fulfill His promise, **but I do know this**: *"I'm going to keep praying. I'm going to keep working. I'm going to show Him that I'm ready and willing to do the work".*

Now, I want to take a moment to hear from a few Holy Rebels I interviewed during this writing process—and share what their Holy Rebel struggles look like.

When I interviewed Sarai, a fifteen-year-old girl from Georgia, she took a deep breath, and her eyebrows knitted together as I asked the question, "What are some Holy Rebel struggles you deal with?". She said, "Living in a community of unbelievers is hard". She went on to talk about how she didn't live in a very Christ-like neighborhood, and it hurt her to see people's lives without the Lord in them. She then began to speak really fast with urgency in her voice. I felt the love and want of God wanting His children Home as she spoke her next few words. "If you see these people, help them, regardless of what the Devil says." Sarai spoke in a soft way of how she hated seeing people hurting or getting hurt, and she wanted to speak of the Bible verse 'love your enemies' in those moments, but she didn't. With passion, she encouraged everyone being interviewed on the call to turn off the lies of the enemy and focus on what God says. If the enemy is saying don't do it, do it, because it's from God. Ana, bubbling with excitement and joy, rose her hand to speak next. The first few words out of her mouth made my eyebrows raise in surprise and eyes open in shock. She said a somewhat devastating, but honest to God truth. She was rebelling for the sake of God- not caring a bit of what culture would think. "Don't compromise your faith for your friendship. If you do, then you're being friends with people who aren't friends with the real you. Don't compromise your standards for some TEMPORARY friendships." Girl said 'temporary' and I lost it. She was preaching the truth which makes me think why do we lower our standards for friendships? Maybe to fit in, to be liked, to be... popular? Friends come and go, but Jesus is forever. Ana then went on to say, "No one in this world is popular for being a Holy Rebel so don't try to be popular". What Ana meant by this Holy Rebels is that being popular is a culture thing, not a Kingdom position. Because we rebel against cultural norms guys, we will never be cool with culture, but we will always be famous and special in God's eyes. If you ask me, that matters most. Period. The last thing she said was, "If you do not fuel yourself, you cannot pour,". We can not get tired of spending time with Jesus, because every time we speak or move we use our fuel from our cup, but if we never refill, we can never pour in the marketplace. Period. I next asked, “Is being a Christian hard for you?” Ana replied, “No, being a Christian isn’t hard, because when you put into perspective, you’re only living an inch of your life on earth and an eternity on Heaven, it’s more than worth it. It will be hard for your flesh, but not for your spirit.” WOW, better preach, am I right? As she spoke and when Colin, a fourteen-year-old boy from Georgia also replied he didn’t think it was hard, it made me think, “Being a Christian isn’t hard for the grounded ones.”. As I looked at all the faces on the Zoom call, I thought that we are all so spiritually grounded that being a Christian doesn’t bother us- we are all too past the lukewarm stage for it to make us stutter or hesitate. Maisy said in a raw, vulnerable way, “.Yes it is hard being a christian sometimes because people always will have something negative to say and it is hard having to see the media mock christian’s all the time. On the other hand, i love being a christian so so much because i have the best heavenly farther in the whole universe and i always have a best friend right by my side and someone to tell all my problems too. it’s the best thing ever.”. Maisy is not wrong about God being the most perfect, heavenly Father in the whole universe. He’s the best of best friends and He doesn’t need a second or twenty-four hours- He can talk anytime, anywhere. He will meet you at your highest and your lowest. Period.

I then went on to ask, "Which of the ten commandments is hard for you to live by?". After a moment of silence, Ivey, a fifteen-year old girl from London, unmuted herself and spoke with her elegant, calm, and poised composure. She was a new believer, but the certainty in her eyes would leave anyone in awe. She said, "Thou shall not covet is one of the most challenging commandments because we can get caught up in what others have such whether it's their possessions, accomplishments". What she said was so true and if we think about it we constantly compare ourselves to other people and it's not healthy. Nor is it right because we are all special and enough in our Father's eyes. I appreciated Ivey being personal, but also being willing enough to admit being a Christian and following the ways of Jesus is hard, because the truth of the matter is, it is. Ivey then added practicing gratitude helped her improve and she found it easier to stop coveting. Ana then added something that sealed the box to this question. "Stop having an attitude, have an attitude of gratitude. Salvation is more than enough to give thanks for- when you get what you want, you're going to want something more so just give thanks,". Lastly, I asked them, "What is one attribute of God that you have a hard time becoming?" Sarai and Ana both said something that was purely honest and thought-provoking. Sarai said, "Probably the hardest is patience because I snap quickly, but I have to go back and read the

Bible and realize how patient God is with His People- it inspires me to do the same thing. I'll just sit, pray, and breathe.". Sarai turning to the Bible for help and wisdom is a pure act of her showing she knows she can't do it alone, so she goes to her Helper. Ana then immediately added, "Discernment- Jesus has discernment- acting out of discernment is hard. If God tells you no, it can be really hard to reflect what God says,". No matter, let's obey our King for God is good, all the time, and all the time, and He knows best. Period. His ways- hold up, let me just read you the Bible verse. Isaiah 55:8-9 says, ""For my thoughts are not your thoughts, neither are your ways my ways," declares the LORD. "As the heavens are higher than the earth, so are my ways higher than your ways and my thoughts than your thoughts."

Before we wrap up this rebellious chapter, I want to remind you guys, or point out for the ones who haven't heard this verse before, Matthew 16:21-23. It blew me off my feet and I felt in that moment when I heard it God had it for you. It says, "From that time on Jesus began to explain to his disciples that he must go to Jerusalem and suffer many things at the hands of the elders, the chief priests and the teachers of the law, and that he must be killed and on the third day be raised to life. Peter took him aside and began to rebuke him. "Never, Lord!" he said. "This shall never happen to you! "Jesus turned and said to Peter, "Get behind me, Satan! You are a stumbling block to me; you do not have in mind the concerns of God, but merely human concerns." You might be wondering why I underlined the last part. Well, when I heard this verse, I felt my whole body and mind gravitate towards it. God reminded me how when we are deciding in a moment of time to be rebellious for Him or not, we usually base it off of 'human concerns' not keeping 'in mind the concerns of God'. I don't know about you, but I want to be concerned about Kingdom business, because that's eternal. Human concerns may last a moment, but it will never triumph over God's. And that's period.

Dear Jesus, thank you for understanding the struggles I deal with. Please help me, no matter what, to choose your words, your way, and everything that aligns with You. Following You might be tough, but the Kingdom of Heaven is worth it. Knowing You're pleased is worth it. Please help me fight my Holy Rebel struggles with Your Truth and Guidance. Please help me to come and lay at your feet like Mary of Bethany (Luke 10:39-42 and also in John 11 and 12) when things are too much to carry. I love you and I pray this prayer in your name. AMEN!

I love you, and I pray this prayer in your name.

AMEN!

Being Bad for Christ,

Sarai

LEAVE IT AT THE ALTAR

So, we gotta keep it real as that's how I do it, you know and sometimes, as Christians, we believe Godly opportunities are **God's opportunity for us**. But that isn't always the case.

Yeah, I know—shocker—I'm sorry. Listen, though, not all problems and storms that arise are for us to fight (just wait for my Christian YA book *The World I Live In: Jupiter*. It touches on this). As you will come to find out, sometimes we fight battles for other people because God knows they aren't strong enough to fight them for themselves.

Yes, you can clap—that was powerful.

Which, if you're like me and find hidden context in sentences, you'll recognize this: God trusts you enough to put you in charge of someone else's storm. But sometimes, **this isn't the case**.

For example, let's say you're trying to help your best friend believe that the guy she likes likes her back. So, you, being a good friend, go up to him and try to get whatever information you can out of him. You say a simple hello, ask how his week is going, and just talk about life and the new movie in theaters. After that, you slowly slide into the convo—light laugh and all—mentioning how many people around the school are getting together.

A little while later, you leave, hopefully with some good info, and you can't wait to tell your BFF!

But... she already left school for the day, so you have to wait till tomorrow.

The next day, you giddily run to the locker with a big smile on your face. She's digging through her locker when you come up.

"Wanna know what I know?" you ask with a big grin on your face.

She scoffs, slamming her locker.

"Yeah, that you won a date with the guy I like. What a best friend you are," she says, nostrils flaring, walking away.

Let's take a seat in the background and think about this. You know you didn't do anything wrong, but your best friend, believing some story she heard, thinks you went behind her back. Now, you can decide to go talk to her or just let her think what she wants. Let's say you do that—talk to her—but she's still upset with you and doesn't believe a word you say.

This, my Holy Rebels, is a battle **that isn't yours to fight**.

Yes, she's your best friend.

Yes, this involves you.

But can you do **anything else** in your power to fix this? No.

And that's when you move over to the back seat and let God drive. **Period.**

Now, let's say you're a rare teen boy with vocals like no other. Every Sunday, you're on stage singing about the goodness of God. And within a few months, a director reaches out to you and says: "Hey, I know you sing, but I'm directing a new Christian film and would love to have you in my production." Is this a **Godly opportunity**? Thank the Heavens—**yes**. But let's say you pray about it, and God says **no**. Yes, it's a Godly opportunity. Yes, it's in support of growing and producing fruitful entertainment for the Kingdom. But did God tell you to say yes? **No.**

As hard as this mind game is, Holy Rebels, **knowing what battles are yours and what aren't** makes life a whole lot easier.

I'll be back for our last and final chapter.

Much love—proud of you as always.

Dear Jesus,

Thank you for Your love and Your mindfulness. I pray that You guide me to say "yes" when an opportunity comes from You, and "no" when it isn't a door You want me to walk through.
I love You, and I pray this prayer in Your name.

Amen.

Being Bad for Christ,

Sarai

BONUS CHAPTER

BATTLE BUDDY

As you get stronger in Christ, you will begin to separate yourself from the world. But one thing we have to remember is that God called us to be *in* the world, not *of* it. Meaning, we have work to do on this Earth for the glory of God, so we must socialize and interact (which shouldn't be too hard for our extroverts out here). Plus, humans aren't meant to be alone. Literally, the Bible says this.

Genesis 2:18 tells us: *"The Lord God said, 'It is not good for the man to be alone. I will make a helper suitable for him."* This chapter was inspired by my mom. She's been my battle buddy through life. I have always been able to rely on her for advice, wisdom, prayer—any and everything. She's always fought for me, and God fights for His children. He stands right beside them and fights.

So, the question of the day is pretty simple: **Who's your earthly Kingdom battle buddy?** You don't need many—you just need one.

Dear Jesus,

Thank You for creating people in Your image. Thank You for loving us enough to die for us. Please help me find people who love You. Please give me a Kingdom Battle Buddy.

I love You and pray this prayer in Your name.

AMEN!

Being Bad for Christ,

Sarai

DITCHING THE OLD, EVOLVING INTO THE REBEL

WOW! FINAL CHAPTER—THIS IS CRAZY.

I truly don't have much to say. Wait—yeah, I do. I always do. Have you guys gotten the chance to see the Christian movie *The Forge*? When I tell you it was so good—it was **so good**. I cried. One of the most inspiring moments in the film is when the main character, a freshly graduated kid, gives up video games because he realizes they are more important to him than his relationship with God. That'll preach.

That's a shocking move, don't you think? He ditched the old and became the **REBEL**. He said, *"This isn't worth it for what I can get."* Being a rebel doesn't start on the outside—it starts from within. We have to have a conversation with ourselves and ask:

What are we doing? Saying? Is it the right thing? Would Jesus smile if He was in the room? The boy in the movie realized that God needed to be his **priority**— his **number one**.

What's God ranked on your list? Think about it. It's something we all have to decide—whether we do it now or on our deathbed. And that's the truth. When Andrew, in *John 1*, sighted the Messiah—the Teacher, Jesus—he ran and brought his brother Simon Peter to Him. *Matthew 4:19* tells us: **"Come, follow me," Jesus said, "and I will send you out to fish for people."** Jesus told Andrew and Simon Peter, who were both fishers, to quit their jobs and follow Him.

Two things scream out to me almost immediately at this moment:

1. Jesus shows how He is the **Way**, the **Truth**, and the **Life** (*John 14:6*).
2. Following Jesus is the most important decision you can ever make.

- **Have you decided to follow Jesus?**
- **Have you *truly* decided to follow Jesus?**
- **Do you want to be a Holy Rebel for Him?**

Do you want the love, joy, and peace that comes with believing He died just for you—to give you the gift of eternal life?

Let's ditch the old together and evolve into the **REBEL**—here and now.

But this can be hard—especially when your Bible is "out of sight and out of mind."

This can be especially hard when you don’t have Christian friends. This can also be hard if you aren’t involved in church.

If you need to ditch your friends and find new ones—**do that**. Being dedicated to hanging out with people who grow your faith and encourage you to follow the ways of Jesus is more important than being comfortable and keeping your current friend's list.

I can’t believe we made it through—**this is Day Ten, everybody!** I pray this was transformational. And if this changes your life, lend the book to a friend. I love you and… gosh, I’m tearing up.

Let’s be bad for **CHRIST, REBELS—starting today.**

Dear Jesus,

Thank you for this day. Thank you for your love and your mercy. It's going to be super hard, but please help me ditch everything unlike you. I want to evolve into someone You are proud of. I want to be a HOLY REBEL for You—starting today. Please keep me and the Holy Spirit, please guide me and advise me on my everyday life situations.

I love You and pray this prayer in Your name. ***AMEN!***

Being bad for Christ,

Sarai

So, you've passed your Holy Rebel training. Well done. But what's after that, you might wonder? Well, rebellion. But that's pretty vague, so I want to give you a two-week plan to encourage and help you make rebelling a habit and soon a *cycle.* Introducing the five by ten by ten-by-ten plan. Every day, spend at least five minutes in prayer. Ten minutes in worship. Ten minutes in your Bible. And ten minutes in a Christian self-development. A few I highly encourage are *The Battlefield of the Mind* by Joyce Meyers, *The Jesus I Wish I Knew in High School* by Cameron Cole and Charlotte Getz, and lastly, but certainly not least, *You Have A Brain: A Teen's Guide to T.H.I.N.K. B.I.G.* by Ben Carson. Now this is a thirty-five-minute plan. If you can't give God thirty-five minutes every day, your daily life needs some tweaking. Now, you don't have to read your self development book every day. Try for at least three days a week- but *everything else is super important.* I also like to watch two to three sermons on YouTube a week, but for now, start with the five by ten by ten-by-ten plan. After, try maybe doing a midweek sermon or two. Yes, I go to Youth Group, but spending more and more time with God individually can't hurt.

I'm telling you; this plan will change your ENTIRE life. I've seen it change mine. If you don't believe me, just try it for two weeks. I *dare* you. You can stop after, but you aren't going to want to, because this is going to make you *hungry* for God even more than you already are. This is going to make you feel more at peace during chaos, more joy, more of literally *everything* (of good fruit). Think I'm lying? We'll see… But remember, this plan is only to grow *you*; this doesn't involve your marketplace duties. You still have to go out and fish for disciples, preach the good news like John the Baptist, and touch people with the miraculous gift of healing through Jesus Christ. Just bodly proclaiming the name of Jesus in an atmosphere is touching enough. Go be bold and remember: **Holy Rebels would rather be judged by the world than be judged by God**. Now, don't beat yourself up every time you stay silent when you feel the Holy Spirit urging you to go speak to someone or when you're too scared to stand for Jesus. It's all a growing process, and the 'feeling bad' is growing pains. You'll get better. I still struggle to this day, and I have some pretty bold faith. I love you and I am forever proud. Be bad. Whoever knew it could be so much fun? Not me… until I gave it a shot. Because when shooters shoot, they never hit the 'net' when it comes to Jesus Christ. And that's the period.

Being Bad for Christ,

Sarai

ACKNOWLEDGMENTS:

Just like that, in a matter of two weeks, we're done. It might sound crazy to some that I'm saying "thank you" for this— but thank You, God. Thank You for putting me in storms, and thank You for bringing me out of them. I used to wonder why You allowed me, at such a young age, to face such chaos. Now I know: it's because You needed me to help develop Your children—Your Holy Rebels—through this one-of-a-kind, adventurous, heart-pulling book. I love You. Cheers to another project. Fourth one written, second one published. We did it!

To my mom: thank you for always supporting me. Ever since I discovered writing was a gift, you've told me to use it for the glory of God. Thank you for reading my books, helping me edit and publish them, and for being there when it's time to celebrate. Thank you for helping with the illustrations. Thank you for being my battle buddy, mommy—through the thick and thin. I love you so much. Dad, wow—can you believe it? We did another one! Thank you for always supporting me and being proud. Your encouragement has pushed me further down this wonderful road of writing. Kai—my little sister and my best friend—I love you so much. Thank you for letting me write beside you. I'll always remember the moments when I wrote while you watched your ever-changing lineup of shows. Your laugh and your smile inspire me daily to use my gift boldly. Thank you for being one of my biggest supporters. To Colin, Sarai, Maisy, Ana, and Ivey—thank you for letting me interview you. That 45-minute chat turned into three hours and thirty minutes of deep conversation. We laughed, cried, prayed, and worshiped together. The Holy Spirit was so present I began to cry, and everyone kept saying "Amen." God is so good. I'm grateful He gave me such beautiful souls to speak with. I love you all and can't wait to see you flourish as Holy Rebels.

Go check out Ana's YouTube and Instagram page: @awakened_to_him. Every week she shares messages straight from the feet of Jesus, and daily inspirational shorts that will move your heart. And don't forget to visit Colin's Minecraft channel: **ClutchGamez**. His videos are energetic, entertaining, and full of joy! Thank you also to Anna—my sister in Christ and a joyful Holy Rebel in Maryland. I'm so grateful for your love and support.

And to my readers—oh, how I hope this book challenged you. But more than that, I pray it grew you. I encourage you: **Be Set Apart. Be Sold Out. Be Unashamed.** *I Don't Blend In—I Break Chains.*

I love you, and I can't wait to celebrate in Heaven one day. There's going to be a **rebellion party**... and our King will sit right in the center.

Being Bad for Christ,
Sarai Lokey

"This book is truly a message that every single teenager needs to hear. The amount of wisdom in these words is astounding!"

Maisy, 16 years old, Georgia

"Holy Rebel empowers young readers to own their faith and reflect on their journey while building a bold, faith-filled community."

Ivey, 14 years old, London, UK

"I love this book! It is jam-packed with lessons in the faith and Biblical references while also being easy for teens to comprehend and enjoy. Totally recommended!"

Anna, 14 years old, Maryland

"This devotional is powerful and overflowing with Scripture. It's truth deeply impacted me and I can't wait to see how God uses it to bless others too."

Ana, 15 years old, Virginia

"I loved it! It was really fun to read and very informative as far as things you can do to improve your walk with Christ."

Colin, 14 years old, Georgia

You weren't born to blend in. You were born to stand out—even if the world hates it. You were born to set things on fire. In a culture that calls holiness weird, boring, or extreme, Holy Rebel dares you to live set apart—and love every second of it.

With raw truth, scriptural power, and prophetic urgency, Sarai Lokey challenges the next generation to stop blending in and start breaking chains.

This isn't a self-help book. It's a surrender manual.

Through ten bold chapters—each ending with a heart-piercing prayer—Holy Rebel will equip you to:

- Pray first, and pray real
- Say yes to the wild call of God
- Fight spiritual battles with fire and grit
- Live clean in a dirty world
- Be "bad for Christ" in the boldest way possible

Whether you feel like a misfit, a burned-out believer, or a young lion just waking up, Holy Rebel will ignite your fire—and give you permission to burn.

Sarai Lokey is a 15-year-old author, speaker, and founder of Generation of Young Believers—a fast-growing movement calling teens and young adults to bold, unapologetic faith. At just 11, she answered God's call to lead her generation with a voice full of fire, grace, and purpose. In 2024, Sarai self-published her debut novel, McVee and the Spirit, and continues to craft powerful stories and devotionals that stir hearts toward holiness and spiritual authority. Whether she's mentoring young believers, filming faith-fueled content, or spending time with her favorite people—her family—Sarai lives to glorify God in all she does. Holy Rebel is her call-to-arms for the misfits, the underestimated, and the chosen—those ready to be "bad for Christ" and walk in Spirit-led power.

www.sarailokey.com - @generationofyoungbelievers - sarai_lokey

www.ingramcontent.com/pod-product-compliance
Lightning Source LLC
LaVergne TN
LVHW011048110826
845149LV00015B/3399

* 9 7 9 8 9 9 1 6 0 8 9 7 8 *